INSANITY

BY D.L. WEISS

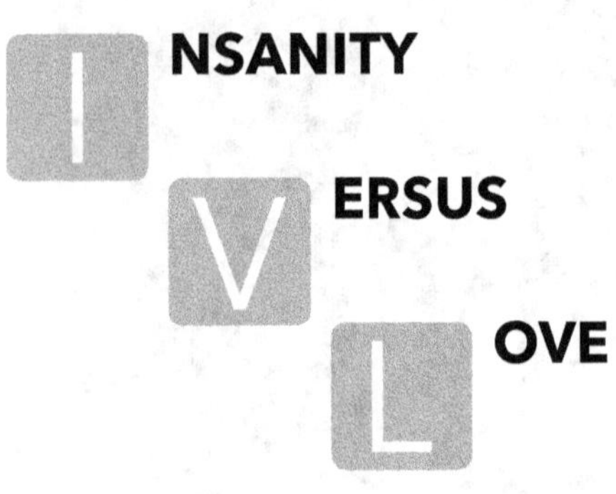

DOUGLAS L. WEISS

Suspend your disbelief:
In youth, run

INTRODUCTION

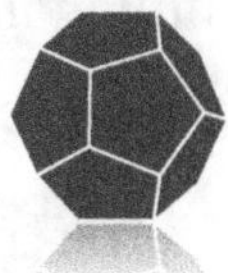

Let's do it again. Sometime. This is the beginning of a story. The same story repeatedly, and again. It starts with the first time. He did it. She did it. They did it. It does it. Now, we can't stop doing it. The description doesn't matter. It's the substance of the substance that is the same. The inability to stop doing the deal no matter what. Let us talk about Insanity.

There is only one way out of Insanity: More Insanity. It doesn't matter the situation or the product of the Insanity, it is all the same. Infinity plus infinity, and there is still more Insanity then that. This doesn't even include people that have been given the title of "Insane." If everyone person on the planet were to suddenly be labeled "Insane," then that would only be 7.8 billion instances of Insanity. To the "Insane", Insanity is funny. To the" Norm," Insanity is Insanity. Who is right?

Let's do it again. This time. This is the middle of the story. The same story repeatedly, and again. It starts with the first time. He did it. She did it. They did it. It does it. Now, we can't stop doing it. The description is everything. It's the substance of the unsubstantial that is the same. The ability to stop doing the deal no matter what. Let us talk about Love.

There is only one way to Love: By Loving. It doesn't matter the situation or the product of the Love, it is all the same.

Infinity minus infinity, and there is still enough Love left over to counter the Insanity. If every person on the planet were suddenly, "Loved," there would be over 7.8^7.8 billion instances of Love. To the "Norm," Love is Insanity, and to the "Insane," Love is scary. Who is right?

Let's do it again. Next Time. This is the second-middle of the story. The same story repeatedly, and again. It starts In the Beginning. They did it. She did it. He did it. This is because the least will be the greatest, and In His Image, we are created. Men and Women, we are created. Thus, we can't stop doing it. The story is every-nothing. What is the most powerful in the Universe? Word. Which Word? The Word that came down the dwelt with us for a short time and saved us from every mistake we could have and will ever make. Let us talk about the source of Love and Insanity: Jesus.

There is only one way to step out of Insanity and into the Nature of Loving: Jesus. The Nature of Jesus Christ is simple: Blameless Faultless Perfect Messiah Savior. There are three ways to discern Jesus: Reading the Bible, Prayer and Meditation, that is learning his ways, talking with him and listening to him, respectively. This is a life and death matter. If we come to Jesus earnestly, and ask him into our hearts, we will be transformed. We will not experience death, but a fullness of life and the ability to Love.

Let's do it again. This time. This is the third-middle of the story. The same story repeatedly, and again. It starts right after The Beginning. They did it, and then it did it. This is because we live in a broken world, like a puzzle missing a single piece. The image is there, but undeterminable. This is about the challenge. We all have the choice to do right or wrong, but which choice is to be made determines the outcome. What is the antithesis of Love: Hate? If were going to talk about Jesus, then how can we neglect The Adversary. Let's talk about the Devil.

The Devil is truly the most powerful revival to exist. None of Jesus' promises are valid if you don't believe; however, all the trials supplemented by the devil are relevant, regardless of belief. We can overcome the devil with the Love of Jesus. When we choose to hate, then the Evil One has already won. When we come to a place of 'defeat,' Jesus revives us. Jesus tells us to live in a good, honorable and loving way as such that the only thing that matters is your relationship with other's and God.

Let's do it again. Finally. This is truly the end of the story. The same story is complete again, and again. It is finished as it starts. He did it. Period. Now is the time. Let us talk about God.

Every paragraph up to this point has been concise and pointed to this one. We have entered the realm of the physical manifestation of hate: Insanity, the physical manifestation of love: Jesus Christ, and the physical manifestation of the antithesis of Jesus Christ: Satan. Now, we must look at the physical manifestation of the antithesis of Satan: God.

What is God? Who is God? Where is God? When is God? Why is God? How is God? We'll start with the last question, "How is God." God is Good. We will continue in reverse. Why is God? Well, God is because God does. When? Then, now and forever. Where is God? He is in Heaven, the dwelling place of him. Who is God? The basic answer to this is the Creator of Everything. Let's extrapolate this one. Time, the ordered universe, the creatures high and low. Relationship between God and people. Forty-six and a quarter years ago, cell phones didn't exist. What will exist in another Forty-six and a quarter years ago that could never be anticipated? One thing will remain the same, unchanged: God. Now, what is God? This could take a while. Unlimited energy, omnipresent, omnidirectional. Simply put, he is Omni. What is Omni is the real question? Anything you can not do, he can. Fly, teleport, manifest something out of nothing, create, destroy. This is what we need to learn: through God, we can achieve these things. Take for example, the first of the previous list, flying. A couple millennium ago, Jesus was the only one to fly, or ascend if you will. Fast word to the most present of time, how many people "Fly," everyday? Simply put, God is Power. Now, we will talk about prayer, belief, trust and finally, Power.

Prayer is the courage to ask for things that are out of our control. Belief is the mental aspect of prayer. Trust is that the most likely of your aspirations will not fruition, but you will get the best-case scenario of all. Power is how God transforms your prayers, belief and trust into reality.

This is what we understand. Reality is a construct or our insights, dimensions, senses, people and places. Prayer can not be fully understood without fully understanding reality. Reality is seen, whereas the place of Prayer is unseen. That wisdom is how prayer, belief and trust coagulate into reality. The realization that nothing is possible without God and being equipped to pray with belief and trust is a gift from Him. If it sounds like this is a whole lot of harping on prayer, belief and trust, well, it is. These are the cornerstones of an even bigger word. Mind this, the biggest word has already been spelled out, Love; thus, the second biggest word must be that of Faith. Faith is dutifully carrying out the responsibilities in trusted to us by our Creator.

Nothing can be something and, therefore, everything can be nothing without Faith. With all this talk about beginnings middles and ends, let us talk about when there was. Currently, there is an Is. Before you can blink Is turns to was. And on and on; however, what was is and will be are the cornerstones to anything and, furthermore, everything. Singular versus plural and then somehow, everything can be anything as anything can be everything was is and will be. The truth of the situation is that there was a time that our lineage didn't exist. What is being is discussed is Creation. It is totally apparent in everything. Before an artist draws a completed piece, it didn't exist. Before a car is fully built, is it a car? As it has already been stated, we are Created in His image. As an image, we are to mirror what we see. If he creates, why then would we not create. This comes into practice in the most complex creations down to the simplest creations.

This is the conclusion: Create, dutifully and with the aim to please the unseen. Love with the respect that we are loved. Fight Insanity with Love. Choose Jesus, so that you don't choose the Devil. Finally, pray believe and trust so that you may inherit the awe and wonder that God so wants for you.

CHAPTER 1

INSANITY

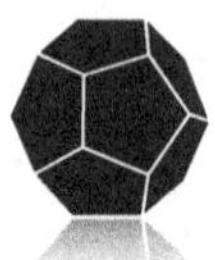

"To be called an addict, or even calling thy self an addict is really no different then labeling certain undesirable behaviors as Insane."

Insanity is usually best described in a recovery program. IOP, OP, CR, AA and NA. The acronyms are endless, but the core of these letters is "Addiction," aka Insanity. To be called an addict, or even calling thy self an addict is really no different then labeling certain undesirable behaviors as Insane. Why do we need a psychiatrist to label us, "insane," when we can eventually do enough "Insane" acts to figure it out on our own? Suppose the clinical definition of what is being talked about is, "Denial." Ironically, the only way out of insanity is to, "Deny oneself" the addiction. This seems so simple, but it could take a lifetime to achieve.

Suppose the subject were trapped inside a room. In this room was only the means to get out, and their addiction. The insane behavior can overtake sanity in the aspect that to simply use the method to escape the room, they could have everything; however, Insanity begat insanity, and the need to, "be insane," surpasses all sanity. How long will the subject be trapped inside the room it might be asked. Answer: until divine intervention, really.

To the insane, this might not be fair. To the sane, this is accurate. What comes first, the chicken or the egg ie, the insanity or the sanity? Were we not labeled and then continue to live up to that label? Why then is it that we are born sane and, then choose to live insanely.

Time has come to discuss some of the forms of insanity. Of the first and second acronyms previously in this chapter, Intensive Outpatient or, IOP and Outpatient, OP let's discuss drugs and alcohol. In our society, should the form of insanity take a person behind the wheel of a vehicle whilst drugging and/or drinking, you could very well be sentenced to an IOP program. The goal is to bring about divine intervention into someone's life, a form of a "cure" for insanity. What has already been introduced is the idea that only Love can conquer Insanity, so remember: you can lead a horse to water, but you can't make the horse drink.

What is a drug? What is alcohol? What is sex? What is relational dependence? What is pain? These are all standard conditions of life. Drugs make us feel good when we feel inappropriate. Alcohol is like drugs; however, all forms of alcohol are depressants. This differs as some of the more commonly "addictive" drugs are stimulants ie methamphetamines. Sex is like a drug but ordained by God between two partners(married) with the intention of procreating. This one is very important to understand. Drugs, pharmaceutical or illicit, are not needed to have a happy and beneficial life. Alcohol isn't needed as well. Sex, between two partners, is a way to understanding God's plan. This is where problems arise: relational dependence is needing to "fix" the other person in a relationship. The core of an AA or CR small group is the realization that those in attendance are not here to fix one another. If this statement isn't applied to life situations, then trying to fix those that aren't ready to be helped in that respect could end up be damaging. The aspect of life that is mostly avoided but cannot ultimately be avoided is pain. Physical emotional and mental pain are all a product of a broken world.

Let's talk about some other forms of Insanity. Mental health is another region that explores the merits of Sanity vs Insanity. There are varying degrees of Insanity, but it's like a digital world. A 0 would represent Insanity and a 1 would represent Sanity. In this world, if a 0 is found, it can never be a 1; however, with a 1, it could at any moment, due to the circumstances of the world, turn into a 0. Take for example a chronic gambler on maniac roll. Due to the endorphins generated by constantly winning, they are doing something insane by making high bets, but sane because they are winning. Should their socio-economic status flatline, that 1 becomes a 0 because everything that person was defined by is now gone. This same example could be executed to someone who uses drugs and has a stable job. Whilst using and having said illicit substances, they may be doing something considered to be insane, but having the means to replenish stores, all is well. Then comes the all too familiar but, loses job and runs out of drugs, and then that 1 becomes a 0. This is an all too similar situation with Insanity. Have stuff, do stuff, have stuff, do stuff, don't have stuff, do other stuff and finally, crash. This is the loop of Insanity.

CHAPTER 2

LOVE

"What is Love? According to the Bible, God is Love. "

What is Love? According to the Bible, God is Love. What isn't Love? Sex. Let me be clear, Love and sex are not the same thing. It isn't required to have sex to Love, but it is required to Love to have sex. Now, with a basis of what love is and is not, let us discuss the antithesis of Love: Hate. Being a mirror of Love, means that discrimination, disrespect and flat out dissing, is inappropriate. Simply saying the previous is "bad" behavior almost gives a pass to these sorts of activities. At times we are instructed to be "bad" when it's our "turn" to be bad. Whereas, we will be "good," only when it is our "turn" to be good. "Good" and "bad" are not effective words. How are you? Good. What does that mean. It is a passive form of Insanity. How are you? Bad. What does that mean? It's an impartial form of Insanity. Good and bad are non-descriptive words used by all people when they are simply in a state of not knowing accurately their status. Now that is a word, status. We'll get back to that, but first, understand that by asking somebody how they are, it should be assumed you want an answer greater than, "good" or "bad."

Status and greater are two words that need their own paragraphs. This is because a status is so much. It is all encompassing. It is the update about a person that should be expected. The first part of every status should be whether they Love or Hate. They Love this, they hate that. The next part must be a because statement accompanied with status. The thing is hated because it is less then what is loved. Further in these works, a more complete discussion about prayer will come; however, when hearing that somebody hates something, it is now an identification for prayer in their life. One step further, when the thing is loved because it is greater than what they hate, that too must be prayed for so that it is greater.

The reason for the importance of the word "greater" is because the Bible points out the importance of such a word. Faith hope and Love of these Love is the what? The Greatest. So, it could be assumed that Faith is Good, Hope is Great, and Love is Greater. Why? Because faith comes from our spirit, Hope comes from God and Love is Jesus.

So, when discussing status and greater, it must be understood that everyone is different. Some are fast, some are slow, physically, emotionally and mentally. What about being spiritually fast and spiritually slow? Why is it some trials seem to last forever, and some are fleeting but so awe inspiring? Therefore, the words "good" and "bad" are basically pointless.

Along with prayer, a further discussion will be about reality. This is being brought up because good and bad a perspective of reality. That would be like saying God has two natures, good and bad. Is that accurate? No. So, let this be a lesson, the next time it is asked how you are doing, attack the subject from a place of love, and dig for answers so that all that is revealed can be prayed about.

Another topic of Love that deserves its own paragraph is generosity. The act of generosity in time, money, thought and compassion are all great ways of showing Love. If this is a blueprint of Love, the ultimate lesson to be learned from Love is to treat everyone equally, and Love for oneself should be echoed onto those all around. This can be difficult when those that are repulsing usually need the most Love. Once the gift of Love has been acquired, it must be shared to be retained. As it is said in the Bible, you must give up your life to gain it. How is this done? By living with Christ in the center of all interactions. Driving yield to let someone into your lane. Shopping interact with the other customers and offering to help them in some trivial way could go a long way. Waiting, simply talking to bystanders about Jesus in your life is more beneficial then telling them the end is near, repent.

Love is the Gold Standard of life. The more practice you have at loving others, the more beneficial you will be in the series of life that requires us to be strong to stand against Insanity. In all things, simply Love.

CHAPTER 3

JESUS

Messiah, the Alpha and Omega the first and last, our ultimate savior Jesus Christ, the remedy to insanity, and Love manifested. Let us discuss the one who came down and dwelt with us for a time.

Jesus is with us from the beginning, through the rough patches in the middle and all the way to the end. His Love is what strengthens us when we can not overcome the trials and tribulations that arise from the unseen world. When Jesus decree's anything, it is final. As he said, "it is finished," by believing (another topic to be discussed), the power of Love comes to life and wears a crown of thorns that show us an alternate way to live, chasing Him versus chasing a dream. We must die to our worldly ways and live in peace and harmony. Natural reaction is to attack when attacked, but what if we choose to turn the other cheek as referenced in the Bible. Offer our attacker prayers instead of off colored words? Give the attacker what he seeks. Not in a sense of depriving ourselves of our needs but pouring out the gift of the Spirit we received onto the most heinous of offenders. How is that even possible? We must heal so that we have the same character as Jesus.

As a follower of Jesus, we are the salt and light of this world. We give it taste and depth that even as a believer, may be difficult to believe and imagine. Therefore, let's describe what we believe and imagine about Jesus to be truth. Three big words with such short syllables, believe, imagine, and truth; however, they are in, around, and everywhere. We believe that Jesus is affording us a life of unlimited potential. We imagine what that looks like and accept it as truth.

Here is a story about potential: We must first believe that something can come of nothing. Something isn't too foreign of a concept, but the word nothing is pretty much incoherent. What best represents nothing is a form of lack. Thus, lacking and then gaining is the best way to describe something out of nothing, and belief that this can happen is crucial to potential. Next, comes imagination. How grand your imagination may be relying on a multitude of factors. One thing is for sure: you are only limited in potential by your lack of imagination. Jesus is as big as you can imagine, and as small as you can imagine. To some, he is everything, and to others, he is nothing; however, nothing is still something, and a lack of Jesus just further solidifies the need for Him, being something. This is the definition of truth. If something is put under a Jesus-microscope, or put in front of a Jesus-telescope, then ultimately every fiber of being is revealed to be an intricate part of Jesus.

Let us delve deeper into the unification of Jesus with people, places and things. People are created in the way Jesus was created, via the Holy Spirit. Truth. Places may be named by people, but they were created by God, who is Jesus. Truth. People take their imagination, a gift from the Holy Spirit, and create things. Furthermore, Jesus is the central key in the creation of

things as everything that has been created since his crucifixion
(and even before), have been integrally preparing this World for his
return. People are born and then die; places are destroyed and
renamed; things come and go out of favor of those who covet
them. All this fade, but one thing remains: Jesus.

This is not the only fact about the source of all life. Life
goes on it is said, even more so for those who follow the path of
Jesus. Jesus promises you will not perish by believing: You will
instead receive eternal life. This is acknowledged at the conclusion
of the three days after the crucifixion. Jesus himself rose from the
dead. This path is razor narrow. All who believe shall inherit the
blessings of the King of Heaven, Jesus: Jesus didn't come to
condemn the world, but to save it and all who believe in Him.

CHAPTER 4

LUCIFER

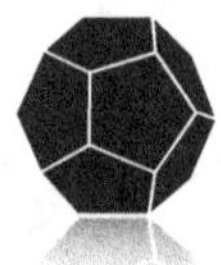

*"What is Evil? Well, you can't spell Devil without evil;
Life without a counter would be a Perfect World."*

What is Evil? Well, you can't spell Devil without evil; Life without a counter would be a Perfect World. We are now talking about the two paths of mortality. Choose Jesus and you will be born twice to die once. Choose the devil and you will live once and die once. Looking the Devil in the eye is like being unsaved, looking into the mirror. It is not the reflection of Christ in us: it is the aspect of our nature that is simply put, evil. The Devil wants you to lie, cheat, steal, murder, destroy, rape and pillage. These actions are generally directed toward others, but the Devil knows he has you when you self-inflict these acts of Insanity upon your self. This is the truth about the Devil: He is real, and really wants your worship.

It's a simple choice, but its ramifications are life lasting. Life doesn't end when you breathe your last breath. What happens at that point is up for debate, but who is debating? Survivors and followers of the Devil. It can be difficult to differentiate between the two. It's talked about in the "end times," that there will be many people claiming to be Jesus. This is an indication of a wolf in sheep's clothing. There is only one Jesus, and if you've heard His voice, you know how sweet it is. Contradictory to the Great I am, is the one who leaves bitterness in your lips. Anything Lucifer offers you is temporary when compared to eternity. Satan will take your soul in exchange for a sack of silver, revenge against an aggressor, truth in the form of a lie and ultimately, the true nothing for nothing. What does this last statement mean? It means that when we die, and Jesus comes back, everything received from a deal with the devil will be given to the ones Jesus has already chosen.

Lucifer is going to hell. We are going to Heaven. Remember that fact, as it is your ultimate destiny. You will inherit the Kingdom, the Glory and things so grand that no mind that has come, is here or will be can comprehend. Do not accept the lies of Lucifer. Keep these facts about him in mind: He tempted the ultimate and lost. He tried to do it again and lost. Guess what, he tried to do it again and was still unsuccessful. That same spirit of victory has been granted to us in the form of Holy Spirit. Not "A" or "The," but Holy Spirit, the only one.

God did not create sheep to govern this Earth, but man. This fact is significant because Lucifer isn't a man: He is a fallen angel and, as such, is less then a man. Far below a man who is destined for Heaven, when his resting place is a fiery pit, to be destroyed. This does not mean you can not be tempted: we have the choice to do right or wrong. If someone dropped a twenty-dollar bill at the ATM and didn't realize it, do you pick it up and give it back, or pocket it? This is the world we live in, and it's the Devil's playground.

CHAPTER 5

GOD

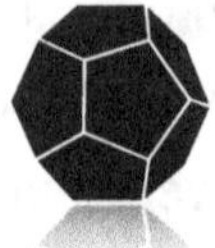

"This is the part concerning the Great I am in the fullest of detail that can be expressed with words. "

This is the part concerning the Great I am in the fullest of detail that can be expressed with words. God is our creator. God is our father in Heaven and is of three parts, He the father, He, Jesus, the son and Holy Spirit. The author of great works gets a by line; God is the Great Author of life, and God is on his by line. Everything, anything, nothing, something, all things, God is the Greatest. Seated in the place of the Highest because he Is! God shines bright at night and even brighter during the day. All hope, inspiration, truth, trust, faith, belief, generosity, kindness, and Love are because of God. This is the image we are to aspire too, assuming that is the correct word. If Earth is one-part Earth, one-part Moon, and one-part Gravity, God is the entire equation. God plus everything equals God. God plus nothing equals God. God plus God equals God. It doesn't matter how you compute it. God is at the center of everything.

Fear God, Love Jesus and commune with Holy Spirit. This is God's ultimate purpose for us: to learn to live as Jesus did, free from Insanity, pray to God and meditate. God is supreme. God is

Sane! Therefore, we are all Insane until proven innocent by washing in the blood of the Lamb. This concept is so important to grasp: God is perfect, and he doesn't have to prove that to anyone. That is because God is God. We are pieces in the struggle between sanity and Insanity. This is the game of Life with us as the pieces and God and Lucifer playing. If it were written that way in Job, why would it be any different now? As it is written in Ecclesiastes, history is a never ending, repeating scenario. The one thing that is always the same is Perfect.

This is the beginning. Two people are with God, disobey him. Perfect is the idea of creating an entire plan to redeem that one mistake and take them past the point of no return. They then return, to a place far greater than their minds can imagine. In this place, there are no tears, pain, suffering or even death. This is the plan of Redemption by God. And it is Perfect. There are no loopholes or ear marks, it's simple, concise, and final. So final, that generations upon generations are accepted and enter God's presence.

The goodness and greatness of God can be discussed forever. How we interact with his grace must be mentioned before concluding. Essentially, we are heinous in God's eye. Then, we choose to accept his Love and Grace. God usher's us into his family. What is Grace? Grace is the penultimate gift from God. It's a showering upon our lives with endless, ceaseless Love: It is the result of our accepting God as God.

CHAPTER 6

WISDOM

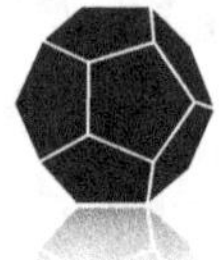

"Wisdom is God manifested in us"

Wisdom is God manifested in us. The calling for wisdom comes directly from our hearts when we are in alignment with God's will. What than, is Gods Will? It means that we have the choice to make the right and wrong decision; However, without wisdom we lack the ability to discern the two. Solomon prayed for wisdom and became the greatest king Israel has ever known. That is how POWER works with wisdom to create a better place in this world.

Two elements are required for effective wisdom: Prayer and Belief. Prayer is asking God for our heart's desire, according to his good purpose. Belief is knowing in your heart that it will be granted by God. It is said a mustard seed of faith, mustard seed being Prayer, and faith, being belief, mountain's can be moved. This comes from the Bible, the book of mustard seeds if you will. The father's who have come before us have shown what wisdom, prayer and belief can generate: parting of seas, slaying of giants and walking on water are just some examples.

Here I must teach you the prayer: Our Father, who art in Heaven, hallowed be thy name. Thy kingdom come; thy will be done. On Earth as it is in Heaven. Give us this day, our daily bread and forgive us our trespasses as we forgive those who have trespassed against us and deliver us from evil. Amen. That word, "Amen" concludes all prayers; however, this prayer is significant. It is called the Lord's Prayer and could be considered a catch all for any need. God knows our needs, and he loves us so much that we must simply ask, believe and we will receive it. This is how we ask.

This is Wisdom in a nutshell. It is the source of life, because God is All-Wisdom. God is not greedy like human flesh, he will give his Wisdom, freely. Wisdom is an intrinsic manifestation of God's Love for mankind. Why else would he give his only begotten Son to save us? This is because he has a wellspring of infinite depth to share with us at the drop of a hat. All that is required is a relationship with Him. This example of Jesus' wisdom: He showed us to be saved, we must be baptized as he had John baptize Himself.

Bible is an analogy for Wisdom as the Bible is the same analogy to wisdom. This may seem like an unnecessary statement, or even a counterproductive one; however, it's quite nearly the most important statement I can make. If you want to become wise, dig into your bible, and it will grow you in Wisdom through your spirituality. In no other way, can you effectively learn Wisdom then by reading the Bible. God will take amount of knowledge you gain from the Bible, and effectively convert it to Wisdom. This is because the Bible may be in the World, its context is not of this World.

By reading the Bible, you will inherit its blessings. You will have your eyes opened, and your heart restored. You will be able to create the sanest works you have never imagined. You will be restored to sanity.

CONCLUSION

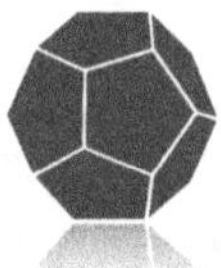

What would compel someone to write a works with the title as essentially Insanity? What would compel someone to call the whole World Insane? What would drive Me to do such things? I will tell you in one sentence. I was diagnosed Insane: This is the sanest work I have ever put my hand upon.

I am the author. And I know I will be hated. Not by a fellow believer, but those in the World who have seen a divine presence in their lives and have rejected God, Jesus Christ, the Holy Spirit. I am prepared for this conclusion. Are you?

Insanity is what runs through my veins; however, I run upon a razor's edge between Insanity and Sanity. I am, was and will be forever known as Douglas Lawrence Weiss. Come pursue me. I have answers to your questions. If I don't have the answer you seek, then find it in your heart to pray earnestly, often and ceaselessly. God DOES have the answers. Whether you like the answer or not, how you respond to the Voice of God, it is your choice.

I have responded to that voice by accepting the mission of writing. The gifts given to us by God are meant to be used to build a lasting relationship with others. I desire peace on Earth, and I believe this was Jesus' ultimate plan. Those still trapped in Insanity, break free. To the sane, teach those that are Insane how you did it. You know the cornerstone, as do I. If there is only one lesson, I can share from my thirty-three years on this Earth it is this: Love other's as you love your self. If you have trouble Loving yourself, start by Loving other's, and soon, you too will love yourself as they come to Love you.

I was taught to write in Ninth grade Washington State History class. I was told to tell them what you're going to tell them, tell them and tell them what you told them. In this story, I'm not going to tell you what I told you. If you want to know what I told you, live and read the Bible. Life and His-Story is where I got one hundred percent of the inspiration for what I've just told you. So, live, read and Love, it's what we're here to do.

LOVE